THEN & NOW

NORRISTOWN

The first bank in Montgomery County was the Bank of Montgomery County, chartered March 21, 1814. It remained the only county bank until 1857, when the Bank of Pottstown was chartered and J. Morton Albertson established a private bank, shown here on the corner of Main and Swede Streets. The bank later became the Albertson Trust and Safe Deposit Company and, by 1904, was renamed the Penn Trust Company. The bank grew and merged several more times before the building was demolished in the 1920s to make way for the bank building that still stands today. This photograph, taken in 1889, shows the bank windows and doors covered with iron bars. The 1880s were times when bank robbers robbed a bank and made their getaway on horses. (Courtesy of the Historical Society of Montgomery County.)

THEN & NOW

NORRISTOWN

Jack and Brian Coll

Published by Arcadia Publishing
Charleston SC, Chicago IL, Portsmouth NH, San Francisco CA

Printed in Great Britain

Library of Congress Catalog Card Number: 2005931160

For all general information contact Arcadia Publishing at:
Telephone 843-853-2070
Fax 843-853-0044
E-mail sales@arcadiapublishing.com
For customer service and orders:
Toll-Free 1-888-313-2665

Visit us on the Internet at http://www.arcadiapublishing.com

Toward the end of the 19th century, the borough of Norristown continued to grow at a rapid pace, with industry of every kind, and perhaps reached its economical peak in the late 19th and early 20th centuries. Employees of the Norristown Brick Company took time out to pose for this photograph taken around 1900. (Courtesy of the Historical Society of Montgomery County.)

CONTENTS

ACKNOWLEDGMENTS

Norristown is a great American story—a town that started with one mill, owned and operated by one family. Since the days of the Norris family settling in the village, hundreds of thousands of residents from every nationality have found the American dream in Norristown, Pennsylvania.

I would like to thank the following people for their contribution to Then and Now: *Norristown*. While some contributions may seem insignificant, because of Arcadia Publishing's high standards, every contribution added to the quality of the book.

Thanks to Jeff McGranahan and the entire staff of the Historical Society of Montgomery County for all the time and effort they have given to me and the book.

Perhaps the most important contribution came from Jack Romano, who some time ago presented me with a book of Norristown images, and when he returned the following day to collect the book, it was then I decided to share the images with all the Norristown residents by way of this Arcadia publication. All contemporary photographs are courtesy of Brian Coll unless otherwise noted.

I also want to thank Stan Huskey, editor of the *Norristown Times Herald*, for his kind words in the introduction and Gene Walsh for his time and effort.

Hank Cisco and Nelson M. Baird are also thanked for their photographs.

The information highway is a tricky one, so thanks to the *Montgomery County: The First Hundred Years* and *Montgomery County: The Second Hundred Years*, *Boyd's Directory*, and Kelly Devine of the *Norristown Times Herald*.

Thanks to Dave Wingeron at Main Street Photo for his professional touch on each and every current photograph. Main Street Photo is Norristown's premiere film processing center.

Thanks to Donna Coll for all her time and effort; without her help, support, and coaching, this project would have proved a lot more difficult. Donna has always been an inspiration to both of us.

Anyone wanting to purchase a copy of any photographs that are courtesy of the Historical Society of Montgomery County can do so by contacting them at 610-272-0297, or go on-line at www.hsmcpa.org. The society is located at 1654 DeKalb Street, Norristown, Pennsylvania, 19401.

INTRODUCTION

Norristown is the heart of Montgomery County.

That's not just a slogan. Norristown has been the epicenter of activity in what was once known as Penn's Land for more than 300 years.

Then and Now: *Norristown* will take readers back to days passed through photographs of once-famous places. As time goes by, changes rearrange the landscape, so readers also will find photographs of what is there now as well as what was there then.

Penn's Land was a gift from William Penn to his son, who in turn sold the 7,000-plus-acre tract of land to Isaac Norris and William Trent. Trent eventually sold his portion of the land to Norris. Thus, the town of Norris began to take shape and was named the county seat in 1784.

Soon after, the county courthouse was built, along with the county's first prison, and in 1812, Norristown Borough was incorporated.

Norristown was *the* place to be for many years to come. Main Street bustled with store after store of fine goods. There were five movie theaters located on Main Street alone. Mansions arose along DeKalb Street, and the population of the borough soared. But as happened with downtowns across the nation, Norristown went into a tailspin with the advent of the shopping mall, and, more importantly, the interstate highway system.

The borough was bypassed by Route 476, and the turnpike exit to Norristown was constructed in Plymouth Township. Soon after, the King of Prussia Mall and Plymouth Meeting Mall all but decimated the commotion that once accompanied a Saturday night on Main Street and replaced it with an almost eerie calm.

Norristown is now on the brink of rebirth. An actual Norristown exit is planned for the Pennsylvania Turnpike, and a Business Improvement District is taking shape downtown.

Through it all, the *Times Herald* has chronicled the history of Norristown in its pages. Jack and Brian Coll have worked as freelance photographers for the newspaper over the years, and this compilation will no doubt highlight some of their more outstanding work.

—Stan Huskey, editor
Norristown Times Herald

Norristown's centennial celebration, held in 1912, featured a weeklong, state-of-the-art celebration from May 5 to 11, with parades, picnics, and religious celebrations. Monday, May 6, was designated as Municipal and Education Day. Pennsylvania governor John K. Tener and Norristown's Mayor Blankenburg were special guests. Thousands of school children in costumes participated in the parade and can be seen here at Airy and Swede Streets as these school girls hold hands along the parade route. (Courtesy of the Historical Society of Montgomery County.)

In 1962, Norristown's Main Street was about to give in to major shopping malls that started showing up throughout Montgomery County in the early 1960s. But in 1962, Norristown was busy celebrating their sesquicentennial as the borough turned 150 years old. Residents of all ages can be seen packing the sidewalk in an attempt to see the sesquicentennial parade. (Courtesy of the Historical Society of Montgomery County.)

Chapter 1

EAST MAIN STREET

The intersection of Main and DeKalb Streets in Norristown was a very busy corner some 60 years ago when this photograph was snapped, showing a couple of jewelry stores and, to the left, the old Grand Theatre. The old theater later became John's Bargain Store. Today only the three corner stores are still standing, and they are slated for demolition. On the corner is a former food store, at 85 East Main Street was the Balloon Connection, and at 83 East Main Street was Volts Electronics. (Courtesy of Jack Romano; contemporary photograph by Brian Coll.)

The first block of East Main Street shows a busy sidewalk with shoppers walking in front of the old Valley Forge Hotel, and in the center of the photograph is the former landmark Philadelphia and Western (P&W) trolley bridge crossing over Main Street. The P&W is currently a Southeastern Pennsylvania Transportation Authority (SEPTA) route that still runs today from Norristown to Sixty-ninth Street in Upper Darby. Today the P&W bridge that once crossed over Main Street is gone, along with the busy sidewalks that were once filled with shoppers, as most of the stores have been demolished for parking garages. (Courtesy of Jack Romano; contemporary photograph by Brian Coll)

The intersection of Main and Swede Streets in Norristown has always been a major hub, as depicted in this 1890s photograph. Shoppers moving goods and taking care of banking needs were the primary draw to the area. By 1900, Norristown had 13 blacksmiths, 16 restaurants, eight undertakers, and 10 registered music teachers in the borough. On the right of the photograph is the Albertson Trust and Safe Deposit Company for all the residents and businessmen's banking needs. The intersection today is still a major hub in the borough but with many less businesses today than there was a century ago. (Courtesy of the Historical Society of Montgomery County; contemporary photograph by Brian Coll.)

In the late 1940s, Norristown's downtown shopping district was booming, the war was over, and young families throughout the county were furnishing their homes with all the latest appliances. On the far right of this early 1940s photograph is Charles Auto Supply, located at 200 West Main Street, and at 202 next to Charles is a bicycle shop. On the far left of the photograph is Kramer's Cut Rate General Store, located at 158 West Main, at 160 is the Firestone Store, selling all kinds of car and bicycle supplies, and on the corner is Schlosser's Market. A short time after this photograph was taken, Chain Mar Furniture moved into the corner property located at 162 and has remained at this location since the early 1940s. In 1938, Paul DiGiacomo founded Chain Mar Furniture, originally located on the corner of Chain and Marshall Streets, hence the

name. Since that time, Paul's son Bob has been running the business and has expanded the store from 158 to the corner of Main and Barbadoes. On the far right, at 200 West Main, is the district court of Francis J. Lawrence. (Courtesy of the Historical Society of Montgomery County; contemporary photograph by Brian Coll.)

In 1880, Norristown was a destination in the United States where immigrants flooded the borough for work, worship, and family. With the riverside mills begging for employees and a Main Street retail business that stretched from the borough limit on the east side to Stanbridge Street on the west side, retail business fronts could not be built fast enough. In 1880, the borough had 18 churches and 18 hotels, and this row of stores on East Main Street that included Hill's Hardware store, Stile's Confectionery, and Lockner Stein's Supplies. Henry C. Hill stands outside his store to the left of the photograph. Today a vacant lot occupies the site and awaits development. (Courtesy of Jack Romano; contemporary photograph by Brian Coll.)

The 600 block of East Main Street has not changed much over the past 60 years, as most of the buildings along this stretch of Main Street have remained the same. Today AH's Garage Sale and Delight Dry Cleaners can be seen on the right at the corner of Ford and Main Streets. (Courtesy of the Historical Society of Montgomery County; contemporary photograph by Brian Coll.)

Norristown, Pa.

This 1960s postcard shows the beginning of the decline of Main Street. Gone is the P&W trolley bridge that once crossed Main Street, the Grand Theatre has turned into John's Bargain Store, and many of the buildings are falling into disrepair. The Valley Forge Hotel (the tall building on the left) and F. W. Woolworth's on the left were within a footnote of becoming history. After two decades of neglect and decline, Main Street is revitalized with the addition of a Rite Aid Pharmacy and a new Auto Zone store. Demolition and redevelopment is a continuing process in Norristown, and within the next decade, the county seat will once again spread its wings. (Contemporary photograph by Brian Coll.)

1B-H2221

This 1940s postcard of East Main Street looking west from DeKalb Street shows several of Norristown's landmarks of the era, including the Grand Theatre on the right. The old P&W trolley bridge crossing Main Street is shown in the center of the photograph, and on the left is Woolworth's five-and-dime store. F. W. Woolworth's was a staple in every successful small town in America. Frank Woolworth opened his first store in Lancaster, Pennsylvania, in 1879, and over the next century, Woolworth's stores would show up in more than 5,000 towns around the world. The Woolworth's in Norristown closed its doors in the early 1990s. The Woolworth's franchise closed its doors for good in 1997. (Courtesy of Jack Coll.)

G 5769 Main Street, Norristown, Pa.

Norristown in the late 19th century had long established itself as the shopping capital of Montgomery County. Shoppers would travel by horse and wagon from distant regions to haul back goods and supplies, while local residents would use the Schuylkill Valley Transit Trolley. Steady immigration and industrial expansion caused a moderate housing boom between 1880 and 1910. At the dawn of the 20th century, Norristown boasted 27 churches, 13 blacksmiths, and 10 registered music teachers. (Courtesy of Jack Coll; contemporary photograph by Brian Coll.)

Norristown's Main Street shopping district thrived for more than 150 years. By the late 1880s, the borough reached a peak both economically and culturally and lacked no amenities. By 1883, the borough laid waterlines and gas mains in most areas and implemented the first telephone lines throughout the borough. The tall building in the photograph is the Grand Theatre, and to the right of the theater is the *Daily Herald* newspaper, S. H. Cope Photography, the Tamsui Tea Company, and law offices on the corner. By 1900, Norristown had 40 registered lawyers; today hundreds of lawyers have offices in Norristown. The same corner at Main and DeKalb Streets today is filled with empty lots waiting for development. (Courtesy of the Historical Society of Montgomery County; contemporary photograph by Brian Coll.)

The 400 block of East Main Street has always been a busy hub in Norristown. In the 1940s, according to Boyd's Directory, the borough had 52 restaurants and lunchrooms, 28 shoe repair shops, 107 grocers, and eight hotels. The 400 block of East Main Street is still a busy hub, showing Caramenico Funeral Home on the right and Lou's Steaks, Volpi Funeral Home, Ronca's Bar, and Giacomo's Restaurant on the left. (Courtesy of Jack Romano.)

The Norris Theatre at one time was the cream of all movie houses in Montgomery County. The art deco–style building was one of many movie theaters in the borough over the years; others included the Garrick, Grand, and Westmar, just to name a few. Located on West Main Street, the Norris was in the heart of the borough, with every means of transportation available running right past the theater's front doors. By the early 1980s, the Norris was no longer showing movies and tried a series of concerts before closing its doors for good. (Courtesy of the Historical Society of Montgomery County.)

Chapter 2
WEST MAIN STREET

The corner of Main and Cherry Streets today is congested with traffic most of the time, but not so back in the 1930s and 1940s. Visible on the left of the 1940s photograph

are the Atlantic and Pacific and American Food stores. The tall, white building in the middle of the block on the left is the old Masonic temple, the Free and accepted Masons were established in Norristown in 1823. Sitting back from the street just out of sight is the old Bank of Montgomery County, established in 1803. The building that still stands today was built in 1854. The Masonic building at 106 West Main is now occupied by Gaudenzia, and 104 is now the Montgomery Housing Authority and Redevelopment Authority. (Courtesy of Jack Romano; contemporary photograph by Brian Coll.)

This photograph taken of West Main Street in the early morning hours shows the Norristown Hardware store on the left, next to the old Norris Theatre, and farther down in the center of the photograph is Blocks Department store. On the right are Forker's Hats, Kahn's, and Gilbert's. While the Norristown Hardware store building is still visible today, not much else has survived in the more than half a century since this original photograph was taken. (Courtesy of Jack Romano; contemporary photograph by Brian Coll.)

S tanley C. Thomas snapped this photograph in the late 1960s, showing Pep Boys on the right and the Norris Theatre on the left. The Norris feature movie of the week was *The Dirty Dozen*. Back in the 1960s, Pep Boys, located at 105 West Main Street, sold 14-inch tires for $6.95, each, installed, and shock absorbers were $3.49 each. The Wildman building, located in the center of the photograph, was being demolished to provide a parking lot for Commonwealth Federal Savings and Loan Association, located across the street. The property is now a county parking lot. (Courtesy of the Historical Society of Montgomery County; contemporary photograph by Brian Coll.)

Norristown was incorporated in 1812 and from the very beginning became known as the shopping mecca of Montgomery County. Stores on the 100 block of West Main Street like Kahn's and Giant were known by several generations of shoppers. Norristown's shopping districts suffered a huge setback in the early 1960s when shopping malls across the region were built in King of Prussia, Montgomeryville, and Plymouth Meeting. The Giant store at 138 West Main and Kahn's are now vacant lots, and 140 West Main, to the right, is currently a real estate office occupied by Maximum Properties.

Main Street · · Norristown, Pa.

This *c.* 1900 postcard shot of trolley cars running on West Main Street shows the tranquility of Norristown 100 years ago. The trolleys were part of the Schuylkill Valley Transit Company. The trolley system that served several communities including Conshohocken, Bridgeport, Plymouth Meeting, and Collegeville was established in 1893, and continued service for 40 years. September 9, 1933, was the final ride for passengers. On the left of the photograph stands the Blocks Department Store, once located at 15-21 West Main Street and founded in 1884 by members of the Block family. The Blocks store was a staple for county residents for more that 80 years before closing in the mid-1960s. A parking lot is all that remains of the Blocks location; a coffee shop and a bank can be seen on the corner. (Courtesy of Jack Coll; contemporary photograph by Brian Coll.)

This *c.* 1900 photograph shows a dirt-covered road at the intersection of Egypt and Cherry Streets. On the corner of Egypt is the office and home of John B. Sterigerc, later owned by George N. Corson. Egypt Street was later renamed Main Street. Today the intersection of Main and Cherry Streets is still a business hub in the community, as a Laundromat, a Chinese restaurant, and a check-cashing business all occupy the busy corner. (Courtesy of the Historical Society of Montgomery County; contemporary photograph by Brian Coll.)

This photograph, taken in the late 1870s, shows Main Street looking west from Cherry Street. Every building in the photograph, with the exception of the Bank of Montgomery County, has been demolished over the years. According to the 1880 census, Norristown had 13,000 residents; in 1883, the borough had 281 licensed retailers and dealers, 29 registered hotels, 13 restaurants, eight liquor stores, and two breweries. (Courtesy of the Historical Society of Montgomery County; contemporary photograph by Brian Coll.)

By the 1960s, the intersection of Main and Markley Streets was left with a few retail shops trying to survive without the benefit of a parking area for customers. Back in the 1890s, this intersection was perhaps the busiest intersection in Montgomery County. A convenient location at the end of the business district, alongside the railroad depot were businesses like the Hotel Hartranft (later the Norristown Hotel), once owned by Emmanuel Brendlinger. The hotel was the heart and soul of the west end district, offering bedding, a stable, and a restaurant. A few businesses still thrive at or near the intersection like Cycle Stop, Finish Master Automobile Paints, Senegal Hair Braiding, a print shop, and a laundromat. (Courtesy of the Historical Society of Montgomery County; contemporary photograph by Brian Coll.)

This great 1940s photograph shows off Norristown as the transportation hub of Montgomery County. The P&W trolley terminal is above street level at the corner of Main and Swede Streets, where

passengers from Sixty-ninth Street in Philadelphia and from Allentown traveled to Norristown where a bus terminal would depart to many other locations in the county. The P&W trolley line was extended to Norristown in 1912 and continues service from Norristown to Sixty-ninth Street. While the terminal building is still a part of the Main Street landscape, not much else remains. What used to be the P&W terminal is now a part of the Pennsylvania Department of Environmental Protection Agency offices. The Schuylkill Valley bus lines and Auch's Bus Service that used to service Norristown are now operated by SEPTA. (Courtesy of the Historical Society of Montgomery County; contemporary photograph by Brian Coll.)

R esidents of the Hooven House, once located on Airy Street, stand outside on the front stoop for this early 20th century photograph. Homes like this were typical of the Norristown structures built throughout the borough in the early 20th century. The Hooven House was later razed to make way for today's Norristown Post Office. Norristown first established a post office in 1798, becoming the third such borough in the county to do so, following Pottstown and Trappe. By 1884, the county had 124 post offices, most of them located in country stores or inns. (Courtesy of the Historical Society of Montgomery County.)

Chapter 3

NORRISTOWN HOUSES

The old Steinmetz residence, once located on the east corner of Marshall and Swede Streets, is typical of the Norristown houses more than a century ago. The house was demolished in 1907 to make way for the Bethany Evangelical Church. Bethany Church was founded in 1845 and previously met in a church on Cherry Street. The church is currently home of the Norristown New Life Nueva Vida Mennonite Church. (Courtesy of the Historical Society of Montgomery County; contemporary photograph by Brian Coll.)

The old Birch Home, once located on the corner of Airy and DeKalb Streets, was built in 1850 by William Jamison and occupied by his daughter Margaret Jamison from 1856 to 1906. The property was later occupied by the D. M. Yost Furniture store. The old building is long gone, and the building today is occupied by Seiler and Drury Architecture, who do historic preservation, sustainable design, and planning. (Courtesy of the Historical Society of Montgomery County; contemporary photograph by Brian Coll.)

The row of houses located on West Airy Street has not changed much over the past 50 years, with the exception of a few law offices sprinkled in. Perhaps the only difference today is that Airy Street is a one-way street as you approach the Airy Street Bridge. In the post-World War II era, automobiles started showing up in front of everyone's houses throughout the country, including Norristown. By 1951, Norristown had 45 gas stations within the borough limits. (Courtesy of the Historical Society of Montgomery County; contemporary photograph by Brian Coll.)

This stately looking twin home located at 829 Swede Street shows a Norristown family gathering for a Fourth of July photograph in the early part of the 20th century. The building has not changed much in the past century and serves as a three-unit apartment. (Courtesy of the Historical Society of Montgomery County; contemporary photograph by Brian Coll.)

The home of Edward Hocker, once located at 345 East Main Street, is typical of the houses built along Main Street back in the 1870s

and 1880s when this photograph was taken. Small two- and three-story homes were nestled in between a number of the businesses along the shopping district. Typically the business owner would live next door to the business, making an easy commute to and from work. Edward Hocker was a carpenter, and his wife is standing at the front gate showing off the newly constructed fence surrounding the front yard. Today the Hocker homestead is long gone, as the empty lot waits for development. (Courtesy of the Historical Society of Montgomery County; contemporary photograph by Brian Coll.)

A century ago, the sounds of horses and wagons could be heard along Swede Street outside the residence of Mrs. Washington Koplin (pictured in window), who resided at 524 Swede Street. Her daughter Linda Ohl stands out on the veranda in front of the house. The building is still standing and somewhat altered, although the veranda can still be seen. The building serves as law offices for Solomon, Berchler, Warren, Schatz, and Flood, P.C. (Courtesy of the Historical Society of Montgomery County; contemporary photograph by Brian Coll.)

This a rare photograph of Penn Street looks east from Swede Street, showing the Preston House and other homes that were demolished to make way for the Montgomery County Courthouse addition. In the mid-1920s, plans were made to expand the courthouse and add a six-story annex. Norristown has been the county seat since the late 18th century. This photograph of the Preston House was taken on November 20, 1928, shortly before demolition; the new annex opened without fanfare in February 1930. (Courtesy of the Historical Society of Montgomery County; contemporary photograph by Brian Coll.)

This 1895 photograph of Ward's Oyster House is typical of a number of oyster houses located in the borough at that time. Ward's was located on Main Street and Strawberry Alley, next to where the Valley Forge Hotel would eventually be built. B. T. Ward is standing at the front door, and Montgomery's Stable can be seen in the background. Before B. T. Ward took over the business, it was Pagel's Haberdashery Store. In 1895, there were 16 such restaurants in the borough, along with 20 hotels, most of which had restaurants or saloons inside. (Courtesy of the Historical Society of Montgomery County.)

Chapter 4

CORNER STORES

CHATLIN'S DEPARTMENT STORE

Chatlin's Department Store, once located in the 200 block of East Main Street (240-252), was a staple in the downtown shopping district in Norristown for nearly 80 years. Founded in 1892, Chatlin's got a well-needed boost a year later when the Schuylkill Valley Transit Company started running trolley cars past its front door. Chatlin's was a modern-day department store, selling menswear and ladies' wear, shoes, tools, and, in later days, records and appliances. Chatlin's closed its doors in the late 1970s, giving way to the surrounding shopping malls. A Dollar Store renovated the building in the late 1990s, and a Rent a Center now occupies the corner. Michael Addesso Marble and Granite World Inc., now occupy the other portion of what was once the very popular Chatlin's Department Store. (Courtesy of Jack Romano; contemporary photograph by Brian Coll.)

Singer sewing machines have been in production since 1851 and were a modern-day convenience even before the beginning of 20th century; in Norristown, Singers could be purchased at 322 DeKalb Street. Lower DeKalb Street was a mecca for business, while upper DeKalb was home to many of the more prominent residents of the day. Next door to the Singer sewing machine store were a number of law offices, including Larzelcre, Boyer, Issac Chism, and I. N. Harrar Real Estate. Today 322 DeKalb Street sits vacant. On the left is Kitty's World of Beauty, and on the right is Gias Agency Inc. (Courtesy of the Historical Society of Montgomery County; contemporary photograph by Brian Coll.)

By the mid-1880s, Norristown was more than 75 years old and continued to grow thanks to the industry, retail businesses, banking, insurance, and the county government. Due to the very diverse sections of the borough, corner stores like the Umstead family store, once located at 115 West Elm Street, starting popping up on every other corner in Norristown. By the mid-1880s, Norristown boasted 20 hotels for road-weary travelers and nearly 25 churches. The 1880s also kept Norristown's 10 blacksmith shops working around the clock. Members of the Umstead family standing out front of the store are, from left to right, Katharine Ann Reifsneider Umstead, and Calvin, Rowland, and John Umstead. While the building still remains intact today, it now serves as apartments. (Courtesy of the Historical Society of Montgomery County; contemporary photograph by Brian Coll.)

Zummo's Hardware is located at 259 East Main Street, where the Zummo family has done business for nearly 85 years. Joseph J. Zummo (right), founder of the business, is seen in this 1925 photograph standing with Elmer Sickle in the front room of the store. Today's photograph shows members of the Zummo family and employees standing in the very same room. Standing are, from left to right, Joseph P. Zummo, Joseph J. Zummo, Ralph Freed, and John Lanigan. (Courtesy of Zummo's Hardware; contemporary photograph by Jack Coll.)

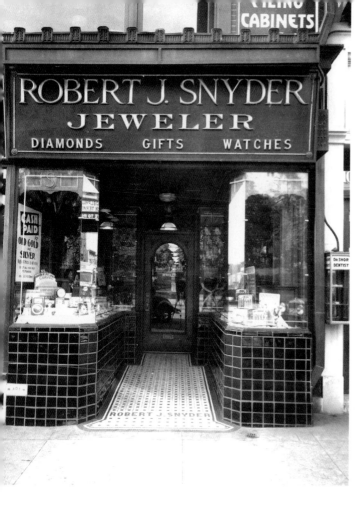

Robert J. Snyder Jeweler was located at 12 East Main Street since 1924 and served county residents for all of their jewelry needs. Snyder's was located next to the New York Store in the heart of the Norristown's downtown shopping district. In almost the exact spot where Snyder's entrance was, is now the entrance to the Department of Environmental Protection Agency's Southeast Regional Office. (Courtesy of Jack Romano; contemporary photograph by Brian Coll.)

E. B. Bickel Dry Goods, Notions, and Groceries was in business long before West Marshall Street was paved. This 1880 photograph shows Mr. Bickel (right) and an employee standing outside the store once located at 419 West Marshall Street. In 1880, Norristown had 18 churches and 18 hotels. Interestingly enough, Bickel's building is still standing today and is currently the Cafe Milans. (Courtesy of the Historical Society of Montgomery County; contemporary photograph by Brian Coll.)

When Hugh Fulton operated his saddle and harness business back in 1880, at the time of this photograph, business was booming. Norristown's first public transportation was a horse and wagon taxi service that transported residents and shoppers up and down Main Street. Fulton's business fell off with the invention of trolley cars, which were installed in Norristown in 1893. Fulton's building was once located at 113 East Main Street and was demolished nearly a century ago. Community Action Development Commission (CADCOM), a Montgomery County agency, currently occupies the property. CADCOM reaches out to county residents, helping them with everything from finding jobs to housing and emergency services. CADCOM has been serving county residents for nearly 40 years. (Courtesy of the Historical Society of Montgomery County; contemporary photograph by Brian Coll.)

Marcy's Water Ice, named after Marcella Trifiletti and located at 424 East Main Street, has been a Norristown institution for nearly a half century. The house was built almost 150 years ago by Patty Current, who was a builder, and, at the time, the completed house was considered the showplace of Norristown. Carmen Trifiletti, along with his wife, Wanda, purchased the property and started selling water ice in 1961, shortly after this photograph was taken. Marcy's Water Ice is still the place to cool down today; Wanda Trifiletti stands out front of the store with her daughter Linda Williams. (Courtesy of the Trifiletti family; contemporary photograph by Jack Coll.)

John's Bargain Stores could be found in several Montgomery County locations, including Pottstown and Norristown. A popular shopping outlet in the 1960s and 1970s, John's was located on the site of the former Norristown Opera House at 67 East Main Street. Like many other borough businesses, John's fell victim to the shopping malls and closed its doors for good in the early to mid-1970s. A parking lot waiting for development is all that remains. (Courtesy of the Historical Society of Montgomery County; contemporary photograph by Brian Coll.)

Taylor's Hat and Cap Store, once located at 84 East Main Street, also sold furs and other garments. Harry L. Sullivan, the proprietor, stands on the right outside the store; notice the three employees looking out the second-floor windows. Unfortunately a fire swept through this Main Street block in the early 1990s, demolishing a number of buildings including what used to be Taylor's. All that remains is an empty lot awaiting development. (Courtesy of the Historical Society of Montgomery County; contemporary photograph by Brian Coll.)

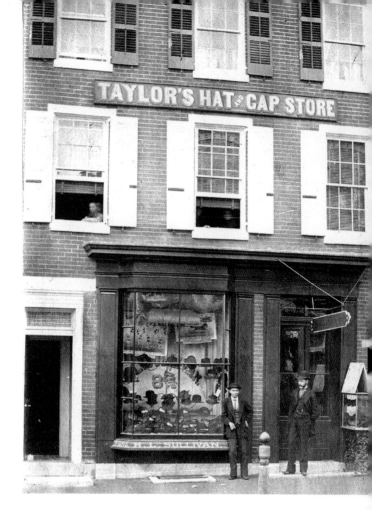

B ack in the 1880s, when I. H. Brenlinger's Store sold carpets, oils, and cloth, Norristown's Main Street was already a thriving marketplace. Shown in the company photograph are Harry B. Tyson, Mr. Frelz, T. J.Gouldey, Mary Fle, and H. N. Bickel, along with other residents of the day. Brenlinger's store was located at 82 East Main Street, where retail flourished for more than 150 years. In the early 1990s, a fire wiped out most of the buildings along that strip of East Main Street, and today the area waits for development. (Courtesy of the Historical Society of Montgomery County; contemporary photograph by Brian Coll.)

The New York Store and Robert J. Snyder Jeweler's, once located at 14 and 16 East Main Street, were fixtures for decades in the Norristown shopping district. The New York Store was owned by Samuel Friedman and closed in 1991, making way for the county parking deck. Snyder's Jewelry is now part of the Department of Environmental Protection Agency, which opened its doors in January 2004. (Courtesy of the Historical Society of Montgomery County; contemporary photograph by Brian Coll.)

Koplin's Hardware Store was once located on East Main Street attached to the public square. Koplin not only sold hardware but also dry goods and clothing. In the 1880s, Norristown was a prosperous community with more than 15 blacksmiths and 40 cigar makers and tobacconists. The property today is part of Norristown's public square, and the Fraternal Order of Police Monument stands on part of Koplin's old store. (Courtesy of the Historical Society of Montgomery County; contemporary photograph by Jack Coll.)

A massive demonstration was held on Markley Street in the early 1940s, seen here outside the Times Herald Building. One sign reads, "Thanks F.D.R.," perhaps referring to one of many of Roosevelt's successful programs. Franklin Delano Roosevelt was the 32nd president of the United States, from 1933 to 1945, and launched programs that led to social security and unemployment benefits; he also created the public works project that gave millions of Americans jobs in an effort to pull the country out of the early 1930s Depression. The *Norristown Times Herald* is the oldest operating business in the borough. (Courtesy of Jack Romano.)

Chapter 5
OTHER BUSINESSES

Employees of the Rambo and Regar Knitting Mill line up for this 1912 centennial employee parade photograph. The employees' parade was part of a weeklong celebration starting on May 5, 1912. Wednesday, May 8, 1912, was Industrial Day, and borough residents were treated to a parade made up of dozens of the town's mills and factories that lasted several hours. Norristown Borough was incorporated in 1812, and in 1912, at the age of 100 years old, the borough had a population growth and demands that led to 95 grocery stores, 48 boot and shoe dealers and makers, 22 hotels, and 12 restaurants. (Courtesy of the Historical Society of Montgomery County.)

The Rambo and Regar Knitting Mill was founded in the mid-1880s when Joseph Rambo partnered up with H. R. Regar. The two later built their mill at 700 East Main Street, where thousands of Norristown residents were employed over the years. The building was built in 1898 and still stands today; it is currently used as an office complex. (Courtesy of the Historical Society of Montgomery County; contemporary photograph by Brian Coll.)

Dr. Bradley (on the steps on the left) stands outside his office, once located at 546 East Main Street. Other residents and neighbors are happy to stand in on the photograph, taken in the early part of the 20th century. The buildings have since been rebuilt, but the row house format is still the same. (Courtesy of the Historical Society of Montgomery County; contemporary photograph by Brian Coll.)

R eam's Oyster House was located at 401 Swede Street across the street from the Montgomery County Courthouse. For many years, judges and lawyers would gather for lunches at the popular eatery. The building was demolished in the 1970s to make way for One Montgomery Plaza, a high-rise government office complex. (Courtesy of the Historical Society of Montgomery County; contemporary photograph by Brian Coll.)

Some things change, and some things stay the same; this old postcard photograph shows the funeral home of Homer K. Dunaway located at 800 West Main Street. The funeral home is currently owned by Richard C. Johnson Jr. Johnson has owned the establishment for the past 11 years, and before him, George Peel owned the establishment. When Peel purchased the funeral home, he kept the previous owner's name, calling it the Bosler and Peel Funeral Home; Bosler was a former mayor of Norristown. (Courtesy of Jack Coll; contemporary photograph by Brian Coll.)

At the beginning of the 20th century, the borough of Norristown had 40 cigar makers and tobacconists, and the W. K. Gresh and Sons Cigar Factory was one of them. Located at 311 West Marshall Street, just off Markley Street, the factory employed more than 1,000 residents at the peak of production. The buildings still stand and have been renovated into apartment units, called the Cigar Apartments. (Courtesy of the Historical Society of Montgomery County; contemporary photograph by Brian Coll.)

CHARITY HOSPITAL, NORRISTOWN, PA.

Charity Hospital, located at Powell and Basin Streets in Norristown, was chartered and opened as the Charity Hospital of Montgomery County on January 1, 1891, with two physicians and two full-time nurses. In 1920, the name of the hospital was changed from Charity Hospital to Montgomery Hospital. In 1939, the hospital completed a two-year renovation project costing more than $650,000, increasing the bed size to 135 beds; further expansions occurred in 1948, 1959, and 1977. The hospital later added a cancer center. (Courtesy of Jack Coll; contemporary photograph by Brian Coll.)

The old Borough Market was located on the northwest corner of Airy and DeKalb Streets. Built in 1851, the market was conveniently located in the center of town, next to the Veranda House Hotel and had trolley stops at each end of the market. The old borough market sold everything from livestock, to fresh food, to furniture. The market was demolished in the mid–1890s to make way for the new Norristown City Hall, which just happens to include a new market along the base of the new city hall, running from Airy Street to Marshall Street along DeKalb. There are no signs today of the old city hall, as it was demolished in the late 1970s. The county purchased the property for a parking lot. A new city hall was

built in 1975 and today is located 300 yards away at 235 East Airy Street. (Courtesy of the Historical Society of Montgomery County; contemporary photograph by Brian Coll.)

In the 19th century, Main Street in Norristown was laid out and built piece by piece without a master plan, as was the case when this stone building was built and called the Herald Building. The building at 67 East Main Street was home to the Norristown Library and Dr. Preston Mahlon's office. The building was razed shortly after this photograph was taken to make way for the Grand Opera House, which later became the Grand Theatre. The building to the right is the Daily Herald Building. (Courtesy of the Historical Society of Montgomery County.)

The brick and stone building in the center of the photograph was the old Norristown Herald Building, also the Grand Opera House and, later, the Grand Theatre. Loading and unloading goods to the right is Wilson and Brothers Harness and Horse Goods Shop. At the beginning of the 20th century, Norristown had 13 blacksmiths shops and several harness and horse goods shops. This site at 67 East Main Street was later home to John's Bargain Store before the buildings were demolished. Today

it is used as a parking lot for county employees and waits for development. (Courtesy of Historical Society of Montgomery County.)

Old Opera House. Now Grand Theatre.

The Adam Scheidt Brewery Company, once located on Marshall Street in Norristown, was founded in 1866 by the Moeshlin brothers. Charles Scheidt purchased the property in 1870 and was joined by his brother and business partner, Adam, in 1878. In 1884, Charles passed away, and Adam was left to produce 10,000 barrels of brew annually. When this photograph was snapped just after the beginning of the 20th century, the Adam Scheidt Brewing Company was producing more than 100,000 barrels annually. In later years, the C. Schmidt and Sons Inc., operated the brewery before closing its doors for good in 1974, 104 years after Charles Scheidt purchased the business. Several of the original brewery buildings are still occupied today, including this building located at 151 West Marshall Street, which currently serves as the Montgomery County Head Start headquarters. (Courtesy of Jack Romano; contemporary photograph by Brian Coll.)

Members of the American Red Cross pose for this photograph in the 1920s in front of Calvary Baptist Church located on the corner at Haws Avenue and Marshall Street. The American Association of the Red Cross was founded in Washington, D.C., on May 21, 1881, created to serve America in peace and in war. In 1905, the U.S. Congress granted a charter to the American Red Cross that required it to act in accord with the military authorities as a medium of communication between the people of the United States and their armed forces. (Courtesy of the Historical Society of Montgomery County.)

Chapter 6
STREETS

216604

This postcard shot of lower Swede Street shows the P&W high-speed trolley line that once crossed over Main Street, went left on Airy Street, and on to the city of Allentown. The term "Drug House," used on the wall of the building, indicated a modern-day drug store a century ago. The P&W trolley line was built in 1911 and currently runs from Norristown to Sixty-ninth Street in Upper Darby. The building today is no longer a drug house but offices of the Department of Environmental Protection Agency. (Courtesy of Jack Coll; contemporary photograph by Brian Coll.)

Marshall Street, named after John Marshall, has been and remains an important shopping district in the heart of Norristown's West End. With buildings dating back more than a century, Marshall Street can be seen with its Belgium block and trolley tracks running through the heart of the shopping district. The photograph taken today from Chain Street shows several of the same buildings, including Spillan's on the left and Estin Hardware on the right. (Courtesy of Jack Coll; contemporary photograph by Brian Coll.)

West Marshall St. looking West from Cha

DeKalb Street, long before the roads were paved, is shown looking south toward the river. DeKalb Street was a state road laid out in 1830 and ran from New Hope, Pennsylvania, on the Delaware River to the Maryland state line. On the left is the Jewelry Factory, which has been there for more than 35 years. The Jewelry factory is on the onetime site of the D. M. Yost General Store, considered one of the borough's oldest establishments at the time, and today on the right is Currency One Check Cashing. (Courtesy of the Historical Society of Montgomery County; contemporary photograph by Brian Coll.)

A hundred years ago, children playing in the street were not forced to watch for speeding traffic as these two children played at the corner of Penn and Green Streets. Lawyer Kane was sitting in the wheelbarrow and the Rush Coaler's shop was located on the corner. (Courtesy of the Historical Society of Montgomery County; contemporary photograph by Brian Coll.).

This photograph of the Airy Street Bridge, taken around 1950, shows very little traffic activity on the bridge. Notice that the side streets had not yet been cut along both sides of the bridge. The Airy Street Bridge was built in the early part of the century and was demolished for the current bridge in the 1970s. (Courtesy of the Historical Society of Montgomery County; contemporary photograph by Brian Coll.)

A vintage 1925 photograph taken at DeKalb and Lafayette Streets shows transportation of the day, including the automobile, horse and carriage, and, of course, the railroad. In 1925, the automobile industry was making its mark on Norristown, as the borough had 25 auto repair garages within the borough limits. The borough was thriving in other areas as well, with 140 grocery stores and several banking institutions like the Columbus Savings and Loan Association located on the corner in the left-hand side of the photograph. The building is currently occupied by Performance Staffing Inc. (Courtesy of the Historical Society of Montgomery County; contemporary photograph by Brian Coll.)

This 1940s photograph features DeKalb Street at Lafayette Street when it was a two-way street in and out of the borough. The 1940s in Norristown were perhaps the best of times in the borough's nearly two centuries of incorporation, with 110 grocery stores (most all of them the corner store variety), 52 restaurants, 13 shoe dealers, 28 shoe repair shops, and four movie theaters—the Westmar, Norris, Grand, and Garrick. Today shoe repair shops are nearly extinct, there are no more movie houses in the borough, and most corner stores have cashed in on apartment rentals. On the left today is Victoria's Salon, next to a clothing store, a dance studio, and Charles Moles Real Estate. (Courtesy of the Historical Society of Montgomery County; contemporary photograph by Brian Coll.)

The Penn Trust Company was located on the corner of Main and Swede Streets, across from the town square. The bank was founded in the late 1880s and was the private bank of J. Morton Albertson, later the Albertson Trust and Safe Deposit Company. In 1904, the bank was renamed the Penn Trust Company. Twenty years later, the bank this time merged with the Norristown Trust Company, and the bank was then known as the Norristown Penn Trust Company. The building was demolished in the late 1920s to make way for a modern-day marvel that still stands today. (Courtesy of the Historical Society of Montgomery County.)

Chapter 7

BANKS AND HOTELS

The Commonwealth Federal Savings and Loan Association was located on the southwest corner of West Main and Cherry Streets. Commonwealth Federal Savings and Loan Association was founded on December 31, 1924, under the name of Town and Country Building and Loan Association. A 1939 merger introduced the new name of the Norristown Federal Savings and Loan Association, then located on Penn Street. In 1954, the association moved to 104 West Main Street, and in 1964, once again changed its name to Commonwealth Federal Savings and Loan Association. The photograph above was taken in 1967; today the building is occupied by the Montgomery County Housing Authority and the Redevelopment Authority of the County of Montgomery. (Courtesy of the Historical Society of Montgomery County; contemporary photograph by Brian Coll.)

The Montgomery Trust Company was chartered on April 24, 1884, under the name Montgomery Insurance, Trust and Safe Deposit Company and was the first trust company in Montgomery County. In 1912, Montgomery Trust Company purchased a lot of ground just east of the public square and demolished the old Smith and Yocum Hardware Store. The Montgomery Trust Company building was erected, and it opened to the public on November 21, 1914. The bank building, along with the Montgomery Trust Arcade next door, was demolished in the late 1960s to make way for the Montgomery

County Courthouse parking garage. (Courtesy of the Historical Society of Montgomery County; contemporary photograph by Brian Coll.)

The Norristown Penn Trust Company was a bank once located at 508-512 West Marshall Street. The bank was also once home to the Continental Bank and the Montgomery County Bank. The West Marshall Street shopping district was once home for dozens of mom-and-pop businesses where residents could find needed services that could not be found on Main Street. The building is now home of Aclamo, a bilingual social service that reaches out to local residents. Although the building has had many tenants over the years, the old banks vault can still be found in the front room and are visible to visitors walking through the front door. (Courtesy of Jack Romano; contemporary photograph by Brian Coll.)

The former Bank of Montgomery County, located at 110 West Main Street, was the first bank in Montgomery County. The bank chartered under the state laws of Pennsylvania on March 21, 1814, and remained the only bank in the county for 43 years, until the Bank of Pottstown was chartered as a state bank in 1857. That same year, J. Morton Albertson established a private banking house on Swede Street in Norristown. The former Bank of Montgomery County building was built in 1854 and is still located on West Main Street but has been vacant for many years. (Courtesy of the Historical Society of Montgomery County; contemporary photograph by Brian Coll.)

A number of celebrities were guests at the Valley Forge Hotel over the years. The Valley Forge Hotel was built in 1925, and in 1936, Amelia Earhart was in town to speak to the Norristown Business and Professional Woman's Club on the occasion of its 50th anniversary. Earhart was the only woman to ever fly across the Atlantic Ocean alone and set numerous records in her contribution to the science of aviation. On March 19, 1936, Earhart spoke at the Norris Theatre, located a block from the hotel, and according to the *Norristown Times Herald*, she thrilled a large and enthusiastic audience with her fascinating stories of aviation adventures. Earhart took time out to pose with her automobile outside the Valley Forge Hotel on Friday, March 20, 1936. On July 2, 1937, Earhart's plane went down as she was attempting to set yet another record as the only person to fly around the world at the equator. (Courtesy of Jack Coll.)

The Valley Forge Hotel was once located at 20 East Main Street; built in 1925, it replaced the old Montgomery House. The Valley Forge Hotel was ideally located on Main Street, two doors from the P&W trolley coming in from Philadelphia, a couple of blocks from the train station, just across the street from the county courthouse, and with a major trolley line running past its front door. The hotel stood six stories high and had 82 hotel rooms, public and private dinning rooms, a ballroom, meeting rooms, and a number of other services. The Valley Forge Hotel was the largest hotel in the county when it was built and continued to be one of the more prominent hotels until the 1960s, when modern-day hotels and motels starting popping up throughout the county and country. Nearly a half century after it was built, the wrecking ball was called in 1974, and a five-story county parking garage was erected on the site. (Courtesy of the Historical Society of Montgomery County; contemporary photograph by Brian Coll.)

The old French Roof Hotel was once located at 18–20 West Main Street and was one of the many hotels in Norristown more than a century ago. In 1880, when this photograph was taken, Norristown had 20 hotels and 18 churches within the borough limits. Norristown was a busy industrial town, with mills all along the river, and had a very busy Main Street. That, coupled with the fact that Norristown was the county seat, made hotels in demand. Today the building is called the French Roof Executive Building, still located at 18–20 West Main Street. Current offices in the building include Programs in Counseling and J. M. Basile and Associates, Commercial and Industrial Realtors. To the left of the French Roof Hotel is L. H. Murphy Brothers Tobacco Store and to the right is the R. H. McDermot Sisters Millenary Store. (Courtesy of the Historical Society of Montgomery County; contemporary photograph by Brian Coll.)

The well-known Rambo House was one of many hotels within the borough limits and was located on Swede Street across from the county courthouse. On the corner of Swede and Airy Streets, in the center of the photograph, was the Baptist church, built originally in 1833 and expanded several times over the years. The buildings were demolished in the 1970s to make way for One Montgomery Plaza, a county-owned facility. (Courtesy of the Historical Society of Montgomery County; contemporary photograph by Brian Coll.)

Norristown was a borough full of hotels due to its many crossroads and railroad stations; by 1920, more than 25 hotels were registered in the borough. The Lincoln Hotel, once located on the corner of Main and Barbadoes Streets, is typical of most of the hotels. A hotel could wind up on any corner conveniently located and offer up to 10 or 12 rooms with a dinning room. The Lincoln Hotel was demolished years ago, and the lot sat vacant until recently, when Chain Mar Furniture built a state-of-the-art showroom on the corner. (Courtesy of the Historical Society of Montgomery County; contemporary photograph by Brian Coll.)

Employees of the Central Hotel and Restaurant stand outside the hotel for this photograph taken back in the 1880s. The Central Hotel was once located at 200 East Main Street and was centralized in the main Norristown business district. The building is long gone, and the property is an empty lot located next to the Duff Company. Notice the hitching post located in front of the hotel and the dog posing in the photograph. (Courtesy of the Historical Society of Montgomery County; contemporary photograph by Brian Coll.)

Hotel Hartranft, Norristown, Pa.

216603

The Hotel Hartranft was once located at 245 West Main Street between Markley and Barbadoes Streets, conveniently located on the edge of the business district alongside the old railroad depot. Hotel Hartranft was one of the more upscale hotels of the day, welcoming road-weary travelers into the borough. Emmanuel H. Brendlinger was the proprietor at the time this photograph was taken in the early 20th century. By the 1920s, Hotel Hartranft was sold and renamed the Hotel Norristown. (Courtesy of Jack Coll.)

The Hotel Norristown, once located at 245 West Main Street, was perhaps the second biggest hotel in the county in the 1920s, behind the Valley Forge Hotel. The Hotel Norristown was one of about 20 hotels in the borough in the 1920s, and as the population grew, so did the service demands, as the borough now had 150 grocery stores and 25 auto repair garages. Retail shops at street level under the hotel included, from left to right, Cunningham's Piano Company, with Ruttman's Taylor in the basement, Daniel Skelly Real Estate and Insurance Company, Johnson Barber Shop and Beauty Saloon, and, to the far right, a Chrysler automobile dealer.

Today a McDonald's sits at one end of the block, and Soffer Eye Care Center is located on the far right. (Courtesy of Jack Romano; contemporary photograph by Brian Coll.)

85

The Veranda House Hotel was once located on Airy Street and for a time was Norristown's most prominent hotel of the late 19th century. At the beginning of the 20th century, Norristown had more than 20 hotels in operation, most of them with restaurants and saloons. By the early 1920s, the hotel business declined in the borough, and the property was purchased by the Norristown YMCA. The organization used the Veranda House for nearly 60 years, before the building was demolished more than 100 years after it was built. A parking lot owned by Montgomery County now occupies the site. (Courtesy of the Historical Society of Montgomery County; contemporary photograph by Brian Coll.)

This 1924 photograph of East Main Street looking west gives a great feel of life on Main Street back in the 1920s. Notice the cars, trolley tracks, and P&W bridge crossing over Main Street, transporting passengers to the city of Allentown. On the left is an ice cream and candy store, and a bowling alley, and on the right is a Western Union office and a shoe store, just to name a few. In 1924, according to Boyd's Directory, Norristown had 25 auto repair garages, 140 grocery stores, 17 hotels, and 65 lawyers. (Courtesy of Hank Cisco.)

Chapter 8

THE REST OF THE BOROUGH

In the early 1880s, Norristown's town council met on the second floor of Odd Fellows Hall located on West Main Street. The decision was made to build a modern-day borough hall on a piece of property located next to the courthouse at Penn and Swede Streets. The new building, shown with the Norristown Police Department in 1887, housed the borough offices, police department, and jail. The building was used until 1896, when the new city hall building opened at Airy and DeKalb Streets, on the site of the old borough market. The original borough hall building was sold to the Historical Society of Montgomery County in 1896 for $5,500. The society moved to 1654 DeKalb Street in 1954, and the building was demolished for a courthouse expansion. (Courtesy of the Historical Society of Montgomery County.)

In 1896, Norristown borough built a state-of-the-art city hall, located on Airy Street at DeKalb. The building was built with two different colored stones in a renaissance style and replaced what was once the old borough market. The new borough hall housed the police department, complete with jail cells in the basement, and government offices throughout the building. In the late 1960s and early 1970s, the building fell into disrepair, and while a citizens' group banded together to save the building, it was determined that it was too far gone and would be way too expensive to save it. As a result, a new borough hall was constructed in 1975, located at 235 Airy Street, and the old borough hall was demolished. The site is currently used as a parking

lot for county employees. (Courtesy of the Historical Society of Montgomery County; contemporary photograph by Brian Coll.)

Chain Str
School a
John F
Hartran
School

Norristow
Pa.

The Chain Street School was built on the corner of Chain and Airy Streets back in 1871, when the borough boasted a population of 11,000 residents. Twenty-three years later, as Norristown's population grew to 20,000, a new school was built called the John F. Hartranft School, adjacent to the Chain Street School, to handle the increase of elementary students. Both schools were demolished in the 1950s to make way for the new, more modern John F. Hartranft School, which was dedicated in 1952. The school closed its doors in 1977 due to the drop in student population. The building currently serves Montgomery County residents as a senior activity center and adult special services. (Courtesy of Nelson M. Baird; contemporary photograph by Jack Coll.)

Back in the 1940s, the Westmar Theatre located at 704 West Marshall Street, hence the name, was one of four Norristown theaters at the time. Following World War II, movie houses became all the rage. The other three Norristown theaters included the Norris Theatre, the Grand, and the Garrick. The building, with all its intricate details, still stands today and serves as a greeting card warehouse, formally a greeting card retail store, and before that was home to the Montgomery County Association for the Blind. (Courtesy of Jack Romano; contemporary photograph by Brian Coll.)

In 1911, the P&W high-speed trolley company built a bridge over the Schuylkill River, connecting Norristown to Sixty-ninth Street in Philadelphia. That led to a connection in the city of Allentown, enabling passengers to travel from Sixty-ninth Street to Allentown in as little as one hour and 45 minutes. In the 1940s, the Philadelphia and Western Company (now SEPTA) rebuilt the Norristown connection station located at Main and Swede Streets. The building still exists today and is part of the Pennsylvania Department of Environmental Protection Agency. (Courtesy of Jack Romano; contemporary photograph by Brian Coll.)

The Evangelical church located on the 400 block of DeKalb Street between Penn and Airy Streets was originally built in 1848. Fifteen years later, in 1863, the current structure was built, and in 1914, a parish house was added (the section of building on the left). The church is currently occupied by St. George Coptic Orthodox Church of Greater Philadelphia. The building on the far left was once Norristown's Bell Telephone headquarters, and the building on the right is currently offices. (Courtesy of Jack Coll.)

14. EV. LUTHERAN CHURCH OF THE TRINITY, DE KALB STREET, NEAR PENN STREET, NORRISTOWN, PA.

Norristown was established as the county seat of government in Montgomery County in the early 1780s. Later that decade, the first courthouse was built in the borough, completed in 1787. The county quickly outgrew the facility, and in 1854, a new courthouse was built. At the beginning of the 20th century, yet another new courthouse building was on the drawing board, and the new and current courthouse was dedicated on May 24, 1904, at a cost of $800,000. When this photograph was taken in November 1928, plans were already in motion for a courthouse annex on the east side of the building, which was completed in 1930. (Courtesy of the Historical Society of Montgomery County.)

This photograph of the courthouse was taken from the rooftop of a church located on the corner of Airy and Swede Streets in February 1929, just before renovations began. The courthouse was built in 1904 at a cost of $800,000, and in February 1930, the courthouse annex on the east side of the building was completed. Renovations have been many throughout the years, including an $11 million project in 1968. In the 1970s, many of the courthouse offices were relocated to One Montgomery Plaza, a facility across the street from the courthouse. (Courtesy of the Historical Society of Montgomery County; contemporary photograph by Brian Coll.)

The former Norristown Jail, serving Montgomery County, was located on Airy Street just west of DeKalb Street. The Gothic structure was built in 1851 and served the county for more than 125 years until the prison was closed and the prisoners were moved to a new facility in Gratersford, Pennsylvania. The former prison sits vacant today. (Courtesy of the Historical Society of Montgomery County; contemporary photograph by Brian Coll.)